# Ten Classic Jewish Children's Stories

Retold by Peninnah Schram

Illustrated by Jeffrey Allon

PITSPOPANY

NEW YORK ◇ JERUSALEM

Published by PITSPOPANY PRESS
First cloth revised edition © 2000
Text Copyright © 1998 by Peninnah Schram
Illustrations Copyright © 1998 by Jeffrey Allon

*Editor's Note:* Another version of "Drop by Drop by Drop" appears in
Peninnah Schram's Elijah The Prophet (Jason Aronson, 1991)
A variation of "The Power Of The Tongue" appears in Peninnah Schram's
Jewish Stories One Generation Tells Another (Jason Aronson, 1987)

PRINTING HISTORY
First Impression, November 1998
Second Impression, June 2000

Pitspopany Press books may be purchased for educational
or special sales by contacting: Marketing Director,
Pitspopany Press, 40 East 78th Street, Suite 16D, New York, N. Y. 10021.
Fax: (212) 472-6253. E-mail: pop@netvision.net.il
Visit our website at: www.pitspopany.com

Design: Benjie Herskowitz

ISBN: 0-943706-96-3 Cloth
ISBN: 0-943706-88-2 Softcover

Printed in Hong Kong

*To my grandchildren*
*Dorielle Netta Zafrany*
*and*
*Aaron Daniel Zafrany*

*P.S.*


*To my mother,*
*Marcella Ruth Grekin Allon*
מרים רות בת יעקב ז"ל
*May her memory be for a blessing*

*J.A.*

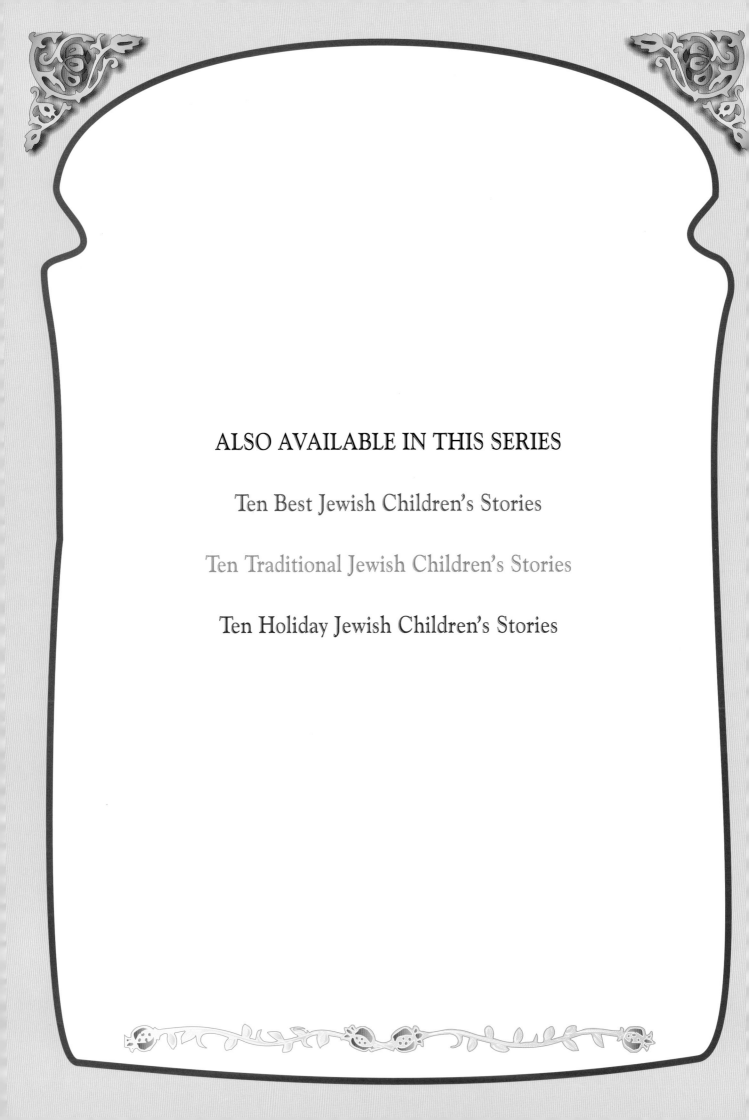

ALSO AVAILABLE IN THIS SERIES

Ten Best Jewish Children's Stories

Ten Traditional Jewish Children's Stories

Ten Holiday Jewish Children's Stories

# Table of Contents

# Jewish Storytelling
## by Jonathan Rosen

$\mathcal{I}$N THE JEWISH TRADITION, STORIES BEGET STORIES. Many of the stories in this collection come from *Midrashim*. A Midrash is a story that explains or dramatizes or reimagines an aspect of the Torah, often in bold and fanciful ways. Midrashim frequently grow out of the cracks that Bible stories left unfilled. For example, the book of Genesis tells us that Abraham leaves his father's house and the idol-worshipping ways he was raised with, but it does not illustrate his rebellion. The Midrash retold in this collection imagines for us the moment when Abraham literally smashes his father's pagan idols.

We know from Genesis that God made "two great lights; the greater light to rule the day and the lesser light to rule the night." The Midrash, adapted here by Peninnah Schram, tells us how the sun and the moon got those jobs – how the moon refused to share the sky with the sun, and what happened when she took her complaint to God. The story tells us something about God and something about the universe, but it tells us more about ourselves, for the moon is a very human moon whose sibling rivalry with the sun is a cosmic echo of the Bible's terrestrial concerns.

What links these stories – and many Jewish tales – together is the way even heavenly bodies are bound to humble concerns close to home. In another story here, the stones that Jacob puts around him before sleeping, quarrel over

which one will be his pillow. Jacob is about to dream of angels ascending and descending a ladder that reaches from earth to heaven, but the reader of this magical story gets to have his own dream, one in which the lowly stones speak and God above listens. A good story is like the ladder in Jacob's dream – it is a pathway for the angels as they shuttle between God and man.

It is not enough for these stories to tell us how God behaves. We know that God went before the Israelites in a pillar of fire by night and a cloud by day. But what of the people who lived, literally, in the glow of that fire and in the cool of that cloud's shadow? In one of these stories, we see two men fighting over a spot in the shade created by the Divine cloud – a playful reminder that large and lofty concepts always affect us in small ways, and that we encounter God and each other through the veil of human failing.

Which is not to say that human beings appear powerless in these stories. On the contrary, their very human scale makes us all players in a Divine drama that, without stories, can often seem remote. Thus we see Honi, the wonder-working Rabbi of Talmudic lore, sitting inside a circle of parched earth, refusing to leave until God makes it rain. The frail old man has the power, in his stubborn devotion, to open up the very heavens.

The Talmud says that the world is a wedding. In many ways, stories are a kind of marriage. They bring together the humble and the exalted, the parent and the child, the modern listener and the ancient wisdom of our long, living tradition. In these stories, Honi the wonder-worker, Jacob the patriarch, Miriam the sister of Moses, still live in the world of words that Jews created long ago to mirror that larger world made by God.

# "Teach Me On One Foot"

*Talmud Shabbat 31a*

There was once a young man who loved to play tricks on people. His name was Barbush.

"Come with me," he told his friends, "and we'll have some fun with those two Rabbis everyone is always talking about, Shamai and Hillel."

Barbush, followed by his friends, knocked on Shamai's door.

"Hello," said Barbush, as Shamai opened the door. "Is this the home of the great Rabbi Shamai?"

"I am Shamai," Shamai said.

"I have something very important to ask you. It's a matter of life and death," Barbush insisted.

"A matter of life and death?" echoed Shamai.

"Well yes, Rabbi, for me it is a matter of life and death. You see, I want to save my soul."

Shamai saw Barbush's friends smiling mischievously and knew something was wrong.

"How can I help you save your soul?" the Rabbi asked suspiciously.

"By making me a Jew," answered Barbush. "I want to become a Jew."

"No one should take this lightly," Shamai told him. "Please understand that if you want to become a Jew, you have to study a great deal."

"Well, I am rather pressed for time," Barbush told the Rabbi. "You see, I want to learn to be a Jew right now."

"Right now?" sputtered the Rabbi. "But that is impossible!"

"And I want to learn to be a Jew while standing on one foot," added Barbush.

Now Shamai realized that Barbush was pulling his leg.

"Get out!" shouted Shamai, as Barbush began laughing. "Get out of here at once!"

"Bravo, Barbush!" his friends cheered.

"Now, let's go to that other Rabbi, Hillel," Barbush said.

"Everyone says he is always patient, even with fools. Well, I bet that I can make a fool out of him and make him lose his temper, as well." His friends followed Barbush to Hillel's house.

Barbush knocked on Hillel's door. Hillel opened the door and welcomed Barbush and his friends into his house, without even asking what they wanted.

"Now, how can I help you?" Hillel asked after they had all been seated.

"I'm here on a matter of life and death," Barbush said in a serious voice. "I want to save my soul."

"Well, that *is* a matter of life and death. What can I do for you?"

"I need you to teach me your Torah. I want you to make me a Jew."

"I see," said Hillel, stroking his beard. "Normally that takes a long time. But since this is a matter of life and death, we better get started at once."

"But," Barbush added as smiles spread across the faces of his friends, "I need to learn the Torah standing on one foot, like a crane." And he stood on one foot.

"Standing on one foot like a crane," Hillel repeated, watching Barbush stand on one foot as his friends laughed. "Sounds like a good idea to me."

"What?" shouted Barbush, dropping his foot. "How can you teach me the Torah on one foot?"

"Oh, that's simple," Hillel answered. "Raise your foot and repeat after me: Don't do to other people anything you don't want them to do to you."

Barbush slowly lifted his foot and repeated the sentence. His friends stopped laughing. They didn't know what to do.

"The rest of the Torah just explains what I have taught you," Hillel patiently declared. "Please come back when you are ready to learn more."

# NOW CONSIDER THIS:

❋ *Why do you think that Hillel and Shamai treated Barbush differently? Remember, they were both great Rabbis.*

❋ *What does it mean when you "pull someone's leg"? Who was pulling whose leg in this story?*

❋ *Why did Hillel teach Barbush the rule of "Don't do to other people...." instead of some other Jewish law?*

# Drop By Drop By Drop

*Talmud Ketubot 62-63*

The great Rabbi Akiva was not always so great. Until he was 40 years old, Rabbi Akiva was known as "Akiva, the poor, ignorant shepherd." He did not know many laws of the Torah Å not even the letters of the Torah, the Aleph Bet. So how did he become so learned and great?

Every day, when he came home, Akiva would sit by the fire and wonder what it would be like to be able to learn the Torah. His wife, Rachel, wished she could do something to help her husband.

"Akiva, you are a wise man," Rachel assured him as he stared into the fire. "You just need to study and gather knowledge. Then you'll see how wise you really are."

"But I'm too old to study," Akiva said. "It's so much easier to learn and remember things when you're young. Nothing stays in my head now." Then he would tap his head, saying, "It's as hard as a rock."

Rachel only smiled and added, "Nonsense. I'm sure you could learn all the laws of the Torah, if you put your mind to it. After all, it says in the Torah, 'Water wears away stone.'"

But Akiva just sighed and continued to stare into the fire, wishing he could learn Torah.

One day, as he was watering the sheep, Akiva saw a big rock in the stream. The top of the rock had a hole the size of a small bowl. Akiva watched as the water from above the rock splashed onto the rock drop by drop by drop.

Suddenly, he smiled.

"It has taken many years for those soft drops of water to make this bowl in the rock. But, drop by drop by drop, the water has worn away the hard stone and made its mark on the rock.

"Now I understand what Rachel meant. I may be old, but I am not too old to learn. By slowly adding knowledge word by word, sentence by sentence my mind will be able to learn the wisdom of the Torah."

That day, when Akiva came home, he said to his wife, "Rachel, you were right. Soft water does wear away hard stone. I know that if I study, little by little, the knowledge of the Torah will enter my head."

"Wonderful," cried Rachel. "And I know you will be a great teacher someday, a great learned Rabbi among our people. I just know it."

"Rachel," Akiva said, with tears in his eyes, "you are such a wonderful help to me. Someday, I will buy you a special gift, a golden crown engraved with the shape of Jerusalem."

Akiva left home that very same day. He went to learn in the great House of Study and did not see his wife again for 24 years. Word by word, letter by letter, question by question, Akiva learned the entire Torah.

When he returned to Rachel, he was called "The Great Rabbi Akiva." He had 24,000 students who listened to his words of Torah every day.

After many years, Akiva was able to buy a golden crown engraved with the shape of Jerusalem. With great love and honor, he gave it to his wife, as he had promised.

And the rock? Well, drop by drop by drop, the water hollowed it out until it looked like a very large bowl. Everyone who saw the rock marvelled at how much water it held.

## NOW CONSIDER THIS:

✻ *What are some of the rewards you can get from learning?*

✻ *What's the difference between this story and the story of "The Tortoise and the Hare"?*

✻ *In what ways do mothers and fathers help each other?*

# The Sun, The Moon, And The Stars

*Talmud Hulin 60b*

If you look up at the moon one night, you will see that it is not nearly as bright as the sun.

But that was not always so.

On the fourth day of the creation of the world, God made the sun and the moon equal in brightness and in size. They were two great balls of fire hanging next to each other in the sky over the earth.

The sun was happy shining in the sky, bubbling, and throwing fireballs into space. The moon, however, was not so happy.

"It's so crowded up here," the moon complained. "My fireballs always bang into the sun, while the sun's fireballs always bump into me. Just look at all my bumps and pits!

"Why did God have to put two of us together in the sky?" grumbled the moon, feeling sorry for itself.

Finally, when it felt it would just explode if it didn't get away from the sun, the moon came to God.

"God, it's not fair," the moon whined. "Why did You have to make both of us the same size? It's too crowded in the sky. Wouldn't it be better if one of us were big and the other small? That way there would be more room in the sky."

"Are you sure that's what you want, moon?" God asked the moon.

"That's exactly what I want," insisted the moon. "After all, the sun doesn't care how big it is, and I need more space."

So, God asked the sun if it was happy being as big as it was.

"I don't care how big I am," the sun said. "Whatever size You made me is just perfect."

"I told You!" shouted the moon.

"But the sun is happy being as big as it is, while you are not," God

16

reminded the moon. "So here's what I'm going to do....

"The sun will stay where it is. But I'll put you where there is more room on the other side of the world. There you will be by yourself to shine at night."

Then God added, "And, since you won't have to share the sky with the sun, it won't make a difference how big you are. I will make you tiny compared to the sun."

And that's what God did.

The moon felt itself shrink smaller and smaller.

"God, all I did was complain a little. It really is not fair to take me away from the sun, and the daytime."

God felt sorry for the moon and said, "Very well, at times you can appear in the daytime skies. But only for a short time."

Of course, now the moon was all by itself in the night sky. It missed being able to make fireballs like it used to.

After a while, it went back to God to ask for a favor.

"Creator of the World, I'm sorry I wasn't happy with the way You made me," the moon admitted. "I miss being as bright as I was. Couldn't You make me big again?"

God said to the moon, "For one short moment I'll make you as big as you were. During that time, throw out as many fireballs as you can into the sky. I'll turn all those fireballs into stars. And those stars will help you light up the sky."

The moon grew until it was its old size. Then it shot out thousands of fireballs. Each fireball became a star.

After that, the moon once again became the small moon that we see to this day. It continues to turn alone in the dark heaven sparkling with stars.

## NOW CONSIDER THIS:

❉ *Why do you think the sun was happy being the sun and the moon was sad being the moon?*

❉ *If you could be anything, what two things would you like to be?*

❉ *Why do you think a new moon appears every month? Is it really new?*

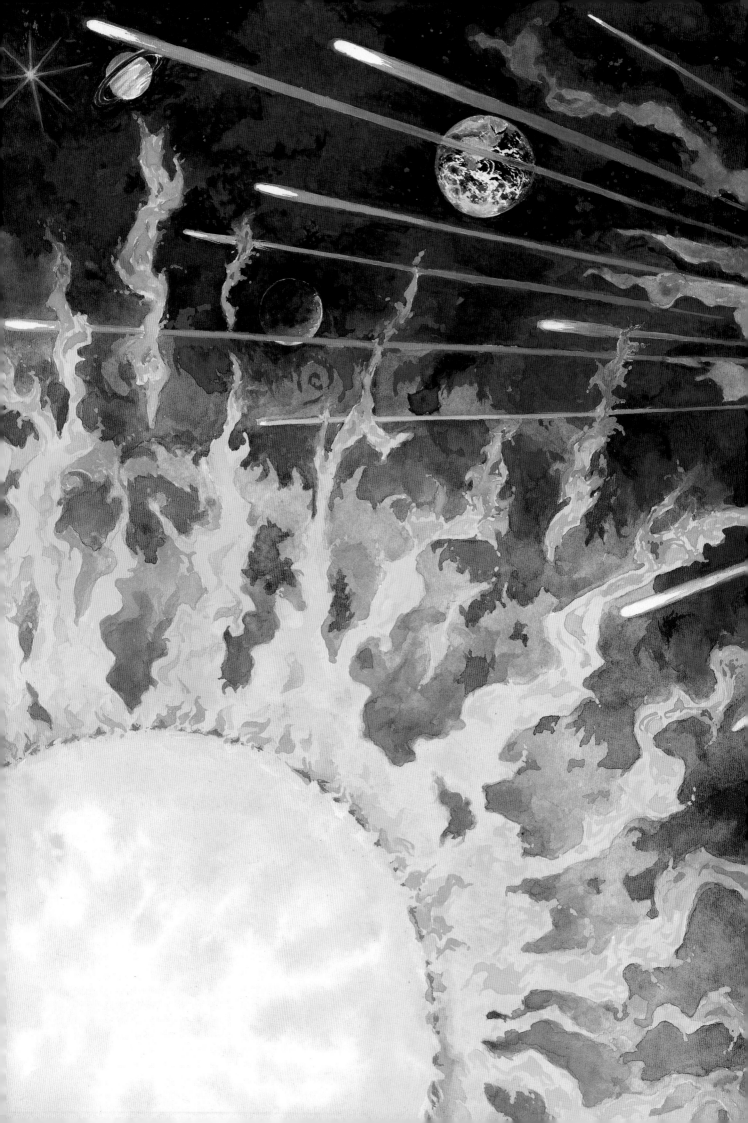

# The Idol Smasher

*Genesis Rabbah 38*

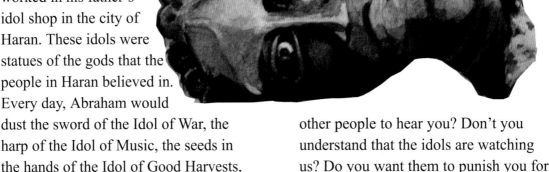

When Abraham was very young, he worked in his father's idol shop in the city of Haran. These idols were statues of the gods that the people in Haran believed in. Every day, Abraham would dust the sword of the Idol of War, the harp of the Idol of Music, the seeds in the hands of the Idol of Good Harvests, and the flute of the Idol of Merriment.

Abraham liked working in his father's store. But try as he might, he could not understand why people spent their money to buy these idols.

"Because they believe the idols help them," Terach, Abraham's father, explained.

"But they are made of wood and stone," Abraham said. "You make many of them yourself in the back of the store," he reminded his father. "And when one of the idol's hands break, or its nose cracks, you put it back together again."

"Shh," Terach said. "Do you want other people to hear you? Don't you understand that the idols are watching us? Do you want them to punish you for your doubting words?"

"Let them try," Abraham said, staring at the idols. "I dare them."

His father shook his head, wondering what would become of the boy.

"I must deliver an Idol of Fire to Charney the Blacksmith," Terach told his son. "His barn burned down last week. I told him to buy the Idol of Fire last year, but he wouldn't listen. Now, he decides he has to have one.

"Watch the store. I'll be back soon."

When Terach left, Abraham continued his dusting and polishing. Just then, a woman came into the store.

"Young boy, I have promised the Idol of Good Harvests some wheat. Please give it to him." She gave Abraham the wheat and left.

Abraham took the wheat and put it in front of the idol.

"Eat, idol," Abraham said, watching to see if the idol would eat. Everything was quiet in the store.

"If you don't eat it, I'll give it to another idol," Abraham warned the Idol of Good Harvests. "I might even take some myself."

Still, the idol didn't eat. It didn't move at all.

"Which one of you wants the food?" Abraham shouted to the other idols.

"How about you?" he said, pointing to the Idol of War. "Will you fight this idol for the food?"

Abraham took the metal sword of the Idol of War and went over to the Idol of Good Harvests. "Eat it now, or I'll smash you into little pieces."

The idol didn't move.

Crash! Abraham smashed the Idol of Good Harvests.

Then he put the wheat in front of each of the other idols and told them to eat it. When they too did not move, he smashed them all.

Finally, he put the sword back into the hands of the Idol of War and placed the wheat in front of it.

Minutes later, Terach walked into the shop.

"What happened here?" he asked Abraham. "Was there an earthquake?" he wondered out loud.

"It was terrible, Father," Abraham told him. "That big idol over there attacked the other idols. He wanted the wheat that a lady left for the Idol of Good Harvests. It was a terrible fight!"

"But-but that's impossible!" shouted Abraham's father. "Idols aren't alive!"

"That's not what you told me, Father," Abraham reminded his father, as he took out a broom and prepared to sweep the idols away. "That's not what you told me, at all."

# NOW CONSIDER THIS:

✳ *Why didn't Abraham believe that the idols would punish him?*

✳ *Why did Abraham lie to his father about what happened to the idols? Why didn't Terach believe his son?*

✳ *How would you have shown Terach that idols have no power?*

# Aaron
# The Peacemaker

*Avot of Rabbi Natan 12:3-6*

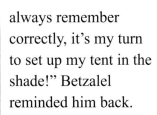

When the Jewish people traveled through the desert on their way to the Land of Israel, a beautiful white cloud drifted above them wherever they went.

The cloud was called "The Cloud of Aaron," because just as the cloud protected the people from the very hottest rays of the sun, so too Aaron protected the people from the heat of each other's anger.

Of course, it was still very hot in the desert.

"Why are you always taking all the shade?" Gideon shouted at his friend.

"You're just jealous because I got here first," answered Betzalel. He had managed to set up his tent under the shade of a group of tall palm trees that grew in the desert.

"We're supposed to take turns, remember?" Gideon reminded him.

"Well, if I remember correctly, and I always remember correctly, it's my turn to set up my tent in the shade!" Betzalel reminded him back.

"It is not!"

"It is so!"

"Not!"

"So!"

Soon, the children of Gideon and Betzalel came out of their tents to help their fathers.

Gideon's children all shouted, "Not!"

Betzalel's children all shouted back, "So!"

Then friends of Gideon and Betzalel also joined in with their own "Not!" or "So!"

The noise grew louder and louder until the shouts of "Not!" and "So!" carried all the way to Moses and Aaron.

"It's Gideon and Betzalel again," Moses told his brother, Aaron. "You better go and see what you can do. Will those two ever stop fighting?"

"I'll take care of it," Aaron told Moses.

24

So, Aaron went to the tents of Gideon and Betzalel. Of course, when everyone saw Aaron, the Great Kohen, they stopped shouting and went about their business.

Aaron went into Gideon's tent first. "Are you two arguing about the shade again?" Aaron asked Gideon.

Gideon looked down. He was embarrassed.

"I'm sorry about how I behaved," he told Aaron. "I don't know what happened to me."

"Well, I've just come from Betzalel, and he feels exactly the same way," Aaron told Gideon. "As a matter of fact, he was thinking of moving his tent and offering you his place."

"He was?" said the astounded Gideon. "Well, actually," Gideon admitted, "I think it *was* his turn to be in the shade. Would you mind telling him it's all right if he stays where he is?"

"Certainly," Aaron said. "I'm sure

he'll be happy to hear it."

Then Aaron went to the tent of Betzalel.

"Hello Betzalel," Aaron said as he entered the tent. "I've just been to see Gideon, and I must tell you, he feels terrible about your argument."

"He does?" said Betzalel, surprised. "Well, you know I was sort of thinking that maybe it *is* his turn for the shade. Would you mind telling him it's fine with me if he wants to bring his tent under the shade? I'll move my tent over."

"Good idea," Aaron agreed, smiling.

Later that day, when Betzalel met Gideon in the camp, they both stopped for a moment. Then they ran into each other's arms, hugging one another.

"I'm sorry," they both said at the same time.

And they remained the best of friends during the 40 years the Jewish people wandered in the desert.

# NOW CONSIDER THIS:

❖ *Why did Gideon and Betzalel stop arguing when Aaron visited them?*

❖ *Why did Aaron pretend that Betzalel was sorry?*

❖ *What's the difference between giving in, and compromising?*
*When was the last time you gave in or compromised?*

# Miriam The Wise

*Talmud Ta'anit 9a*

*A well of water traveled with the Children of Israel as they wandered through the desert. Whenever they were thirsty, they could draw from the well and drink the fresh water. It would give them the strength to go on.*

*This well was called "Miriam's Well," because, when the Egyptians were making life bitter for the Jewish people, Miriam gave them new strength and new hope.*

"Pharaoh, listen to me," said the king's chief magician. "I see in the stars that a leader will be born to the Children of Israel. He will take them out of Egypt, and he will destroy you and all your armies!"

"Do you know when he will be born?" asked Pharaoh.

"Soon, Your Majesty," the chief magician told him. "Perhaps this month. Certainly within the year."

Pharaoh immediately wrote a decree which said, "All the newborn boys of the Children of Israel must be killed as soon as they are born."

When Amram, Miriam's father, heard the decree, he became very sad.

"What is it, Amram?" asked Yocheved, his wife. "I have never seen you so upset before."

"Haven't you heard? Pharaoh has made another terrible decree. He has ordered that all the baby boys born among our people are to be killed.

"What's the use of going on, Yocheved?" Amram cried. "What's the use of raising a family in such a terrible country?"

"Things will get better," Yocheved told him. "Miriam just came home with wonderful news. Soon a child will be born who will one day lead us out of Egypt."

"These are only rumors, Yocheved," Amram said. "How can you believe them? Let me speak to Miriam."

When Miriam went in to see her

father, she was nervous. She knew that her father would not believe the stories about a leader taking everyone out of Egypt.

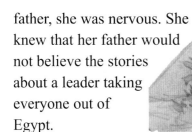

"Did you tell your mother about a leader who will one day take our people out of Egypt?" Amram asked his daughter.

"Yes, father," she replied.

"Miriam, don't you understand that these are just stories?" Amram scolded. "There will be no leader. Just today, Pharaoh decreed that all our newborn male children are to be killed."

"But our people cannot give up," Miriam pleaded. "We must show Pharaoh that he can't stop us from leaving Egypt. Our leader will be born. He *must* be born, father."

"But you don't understand, Miriam. What sense does it make to have children if Pharaoh will then kill them?"

"He will not kill them all. We will hide them."

"Do you think you are more cunning than Pharaoh and his spies? They will know when a boy is born and kill him."

"We won't let them, father," Miriam insisted.

"Well, I won't have any more children," Amram announced, annoyed at his daughter.

"Then you are making things even worse," Miriam cried.

"How dare you talk to me like that!" Amram rose, with anger in his eyes.

"I'm sorry, father," Miriam said. "But Pharaoh has ordered that the baby boys be killed. If you refuse to have anymore children, and others follow your example, there will be no more boy *or girl* babies. It will be the end of our people!"

For a second, Amram didn't know what to say. Then he realized that Miriam was right.

"My daughter," he said proudly, hugging Miriam, "you are very wise."

Amram and Yocheved had another child. His name was Moses. And, just as Miriam predicted, they were able to hide him from Pharaoh's spies. He grew up and took the Children of Israel out of Egypt.

# NOW CONSIDER THIS:

✳ *How would you tell your parents if you thought they were doing something wrong?*

✳ *How does this story show us that Miriam gave the Jewish people the strength to go on?*

✳ *When did the warning of Pharaoh's chief magician come true?*

# The Stone Pillow

*Talmud Hulin 91b*

Yaacov was on his way to his uncle, Lavan. He was tired and lonely, and in need of a good night's sleep. When the sun set, Yaacov chose a nice, quiet spot to make camp.

"The first thing I have to do," Yaacov thought, "is find some small stones. I'll put them around me so that if an animal comes too near, I'll hear it as it scurries over the stones."

Yaacov chose twelve very nice, almost round, stones. Eleven he put around himself and the twelfth he used as a pillow.

Exhausted, he went to sleep.

While Yaacov was dreaming of ladders and angels, the stones that he had placed around him began to argue.

"Why does Red Rock get to rest under Yaacov's head?" Gray Rock grumbled, leaning toward Red Rock who was nestled cozily under Yaacov's head.

"What's the matter with me?" interrupted Brown Rock, twirling around to show off his deep brown color. "Such a great man as Yaacov should be resting on me."

"Is that true?" joined in Black Rock, the largest of all the rocks. "A head as beautiful as that deserves to have plenty of room for moving around. I'm the biggest here. I should be under his head."

"Big?" laughed Yellow Rock. "You think big means anything? Let me tell you, someone like Yaacov should be lying on a smooth yellow stone that would let his head glide across it."

"Well, Yaacov chose me, didn't he?" Red Rock said snootily. "And so I get to have his lovely head on me."

God noticed the argument among the stones, but was not angry with them. Actually, God was quite pleased.

"Stones," God called to them. "Stones, I understand that each of you wants to be Yaacov's pillow."

"That's true," all the stones said.

"But Yaacov chose me," Red Rock

reminded everyone.

"You're right, Red Rock," God told him. "But if Yaacov had known how much all of you wanted to be his pillow, I'm sure he would have chosen all of you."

"Creator of the Universe, what You say is true, of course," Red Rock admitted. "I am a fortunate stone."

"Well, let's see if you can't all be fortunate stones," God announced.

In the blink of an eye, all the stones melted into each other. Red Rock and Black Rock, Gray Rock and Green Rock, Brown Rock and Yellow Rock, along with the other rocks all became one.

"How's that?" God asked, as they settled in under Yaacov's head.

"Wonderful! It feels so good to be together!" they all shouted.

When the sun rose, Yaacov awoke. He stood up, looked around, and noticed that all the stones he had put around him for protection were gone.

Then he looked down at the stone he had used as a pillow. It was large and smooth and beautiful. And it had all the colors of the rainbow mixed up in it.

"Strange," Yaacov thought. "I was sure I put a small red stone under my head last night. No wonder I feel so refreshed. I was fortunate to have such a splendid stone as a pillow."

"We're all fortunate," shouted the Many-Colored Rock.

But, of course, only God could hear it.

## NOW CONSIDER THIS:

✳ *Why do you think the stones wanted to be Yaacov's pillow?*

✳ *Have you ever tried very hard to make someone happy? What did you do?*

✳ *What was so interesting about Yaacov's dream?*

# Honi The Rainmaker

*Talmud Ta'anit 23a*

A long time ago, in the Land of Israel, the rain did not fall from the clouds for many months.

Without rain, the crops in the fields began to shrivel. Without rain, the streams and rivers dried up. Without rain, the animals did not have water to drink and so they were very thirsty. There was almost no water left in all of Israel.

The great Rabbis told everyone to pray to God. Only God could make the clouds release their water.

People prayed for days. But still, the clouds just hung in the sky, not allowing even one drop of water to fall to the ground.

"What shall we do?" the people asked the Rabbis. "We must have water, or else our animals will die. Soon, we won't have enough water for our families!"

Finally, the Rabbis thought of what to do. They sent a message to Honi the Wise One to come. "He will do something that will make God listen to our prayers for rain," they told the people. "He is the holiest man in Israel."

When Honi arrived, he immediately took a stick and drew a circle in the ground. A perfectly round circle. Then he stepped inside the circle.

"God, I promise," Honi said, looking up at the sky, "I promise that I will not leave this circle until the clouds let their rain pour onto the ground."

Everyone was terribly worried about Honi. They knew that if he stayed out in the sun all day and in the cold all night, Honi would become ill. After all, he was an old man.

But Honi would not leave the circle. He had promised to stay in the circle until the rains came. And everyone knew that Honi would never break his word.

God must have been worried about

Honi, too, because after a while, little drops of rain began to pitter patter onto the dry land.

"Honi," his students called to him, "you can leave the circle now. It's raining!"

But Honi knew that these few drops were not enough to save the crops, the animals, and the families who needed water.

"I will stay here until we get real rain," he told his students, "rain that will wet the land and make our people happy."

As he spoke these words, the clouds opened up and poured their water onto the land. Each drop of rain was bigger than an ostrich egg.

"This is terrible," shouted his students. "There will be floods everywhere. People will have to leave their homes and run to the hills. Please, Honi, please stop the rain."

Honi shouted up at the sky, "Creator of the World, I won't leave until You send a good rain. Not drops. Not floods. Just regular rain."

God heard Honi, and commanded the clouds to give just the right amount of rain. Not too little and not too much.

And of course, the clouds listened.

When Honi saw that the rain was coming down, not too slowly and not too fast, he smiled, stepped out of the circle, and returned home.

The people went back to their homes, too.

Only the perfectly round magic circle remained where it was.

And it's still there, waiting for Honi, just in case the clouds ever refuse to give their rain again.

## NOW CONSIDER THIS:

✳ *Why did the Rabbis choose Honi to pray for rain?*

✳ *Why do you think the clouds would not give their rain?*

✳ *Besides standing in the magic circle, what else do you think Honi did to convince God to make it rain?*

# The Power Of The Tongue

*Proverbs 18:3a*

The king of Persia became very sick. His doctors told him that the only thing that could cure him was to drink the milk of a lioness. Otherwise, he would surely die.

The king sent messengers throughout his land. They told the people, "Whoever brings the king milk from a lioness will be richly rewarded."

A man named Mordechai heard the proclamation and decided to find the milk of a lioness. After many days of wandering, he found a lioness with three little cubs. He knew that if he approached her, she would attack him. But he had a plan.

In the morning, Mordechai threw some goat meat to the lioness. She ate it hungrily, keeping an eye on him. The next day, Mordechai again threw her some goat meat. And the next day. And the next. After a while, the lioness was used to him and he was able to get close to her.

Finally, one day, after her cubs finished nursing from her, the lioness let Mordechai take whatever milk was left.

Mordechai was thrilled. But, on his way back to the palace, the different parts of Mordechai's body started an argument. Each part of his body thought that it was the most important.

"You are all fortunate that I was able to spot the lioness," the eyes bragged. "Otherwise, we would never have taken the milk."

"Perhaps," said the ears. "But if you remember, I heard the lioness growl in the tall bushes. Without me, we would never have known where to look."

"But without me," declared the feet, "you would never have been able to reach the lioness."

"Well, I milked her," the hands said. "Without me, we would have no milk in the jar."

"I think – " the tongue began. But the others hushed him.

"You're always talking," they scolded. "You had nothing to do with any of this," they insisted.

When Mordechai returned with the milk, he was immediately brought before the king.

"Your Majesty," Mordechai announced, "I have brought you what you asked for. Here," Mordechai said, holding up the jar, "is the milk of a baboon that – "

"What? Baboon milk!" shouted the king. "How dare you make fun of your king! Take him out," the king commanded his soldiers, "and hang him!"

The parts of Mordechai's body were terrified.

The eyes could see the hangman's noose outside the palace. The ears could hear the command for the hangman to get ready. The hands could feel the grip of the soldiers. And the feet knew there was nowhere to run.

"Do you understand now?" asked the tongue. "With one word, and in one second, I can change what all of you have worked so hard to do for days.

Which one of us is the most important part of the body now?"

"You are," all the parts of the body agreed. "Please help us."

"Your Majesty," Mordechai called out. "I was so anxious for you to receive the milk, I stumbled over my words. This is the milk of a lioness, Your Majesty. It will heal you."

The king had his doctors test the milk.

"It is indeed the milk of a lioness, Your Majesty," they said.

The king drank the milk and became well again. Mordechai received a wonderful reward. But the tongue's reward was even greater. From that time on, all the parts of the body readily agreed, "The tongue has the greatest power to destroy a person, and to save him."

# NOW CONSIDER THIS:

❋ *Which part of the body do you think is the most important? Why?*

❋ *What other Mordechai do you know of who lived in Persia?*

*What reward did that other Mordechai receive from the king of Persia?*

❋ *How would you have taken the milk from the lioness?*

# The Bitter And The Sweet

*Folk Tale*

**M**any years ago, on the first night of Passover, the people in the village of Ashdod were all sitting down to their Seder. Nissim, the town beggar, had been eagerly awaiting the Passover feast. In his mind, he was considering which family to visit for the meal, when a beggar from a neighboring village approached him.

"Hello, I'm Plini," the beggar announced. "They tell me you're the official beggar in this town. Perhaps you could tell me where I could go for a good meal. I've been traveling all day and have had nothing to eat."

"You're in luck, my friend," Nissim told him. "Tonight is the Jewish holiday of Passover, and everyone opens their doors to the poor. You will feast as you have never feasted before!"

"But I am not a Jew," Plini told Nissim. "Will the people still allow me to eat with them?"

"Oh, my friend, let me tell you, tonight everyone is welcome, Jew and non-Jew. The doors are flung wide open and people shout out for strangers and beggars to come as guests and join them."

Plini's face beamed. "It's hard to believe. I have never heard of such a thing."

"I'll tell you what," Nissim said to Plini. "At the end of the evening, let's meet right here, and then you tell me if I was right or not."

So Nissim and Plini waited until the doors of the houses were opened. Sure enough, each one was welcomed to a Seder.

Around midnight, Nissim made his way back to meet Plini. He could barely walk straight from drinking so much wine. His stomach was full from the delicious food he had eaten. The crispy matza left a wonderful taste in his mouth.

But when he arrived at their meeting place, Nissim was amazed to see Plini pacing back and forth, mumbling to himself.

"You!" Plini shouted when he saw

44

Nissim. "You lied to me!"

"What do you mean?"Asked Nissim, bewildered. "Was it not everything I told you?"

"What? After what I have just been through, I realize I was a fool to believe you!"

"What happened?" Nissim asked. "Tell me."

"Well, I was welcomed into the family's house, just as you said," Plini admitted, "and I could smell the delicious food throughout the house. I was almost dizzy from hunger.

"But there was very little food on the table. Just some thin, crusty bread that everyone called matza, and little bits of food on a plate, barely enough for one person.

"Then everyone began to ask questions and talk, and talk, and talk. For hours they talked. Children talked. Grownups talked. They even wanted me to talk, but what could I say?

"Finally, the talking ended. I was starving."

"So then you began to feast," Nissim interrupted.

"Feast? What feast? They gave me some of the matza with some white stuff on it. I took one bite and let out a yell that made everyone laugh. It was horseradish! The most bitter thing I have ever eaten. I got up and ran out the door."

Nissim realized what had happened, and felt sorry for Plini.

"Plini, my friend," he said. "That was the beginning of the meal. The horseradish reminds us of our hard life in Egypt. But you should have waited for the bitterness to pass. Then you would have enjoyed all the sweet and delicious foods that are brought out to remind us of the freedom that came afterwards."

# NOW CONSIDER THIS:

✳ *What experiences sometimes hurt, but then make you feel better?*

✳ *If Plini had come to your Seder, how would you have explained the horseradish to him?*

✳ *Why do Jews want guests to come to their Seder?*